SPEC. 14

MANUAL
of
HERPETOLOGY

JOAN PROCTER, DRAGON DOCTOR

THE WOMAN WHO LOVED REPTILES

SPECIMEN
2·B

Written by

Patricia Valdez

Illustrated by

Felicita Sala

ALFRED A. KNOPF

New York

For Mateo and Maya, may you always be fearless
—P.V.

For Samuele, the scientist
—F.S.

THIS IS A BORZOI BOOK PUBLISHED BY ALFRED A. KNOPF

Text copyright © 2018 by Patricia Valdez
Jacket art and interior illustrations copyright © 2018 by Felicita Sala

All rights reserved. Published in the United States by Alfred A. Knopf, an imprint of
Random House Children's Books, a division of Penguin Random House LLC, New York.

Photo of Joan Procter and Ramases copyright © the Mistresses and Fellows, Girton College, Cambridge
Photo of Joan Procter © the Zoological Society of London
Photos of Joan Procter's paintings © the Zoological Society of London

Visit us on the Web! randomhousekids.com

Educators and librarians, for a variety of teaching tools, visit us at RHTeachersLibrarians.com

Library of Congress Cataloging-in-Publication Data is available upon request.
ISBN 978-0-399-55725-5 (trade) — ISBN 978-0-399-55726-2 (lib. bdg.) — ISBN 978-0-399-55727-9 (ebook)

MANUFACTURED IN CHINA
March 2018
10 9 8 7 6 5 4

First Edition

Back in the days of long skirts and afternoon teas, a little girl named Joan Procter entertained the most unusual party guests.

Slithery and scaly, they turned over teacups. They crawled past the crumpets.

While other girls read stories about dragons and princesses, Joan read books about lizards and crocodiles. Instead of a favorite doll, a favorite lizard accompanied her wherever she went.

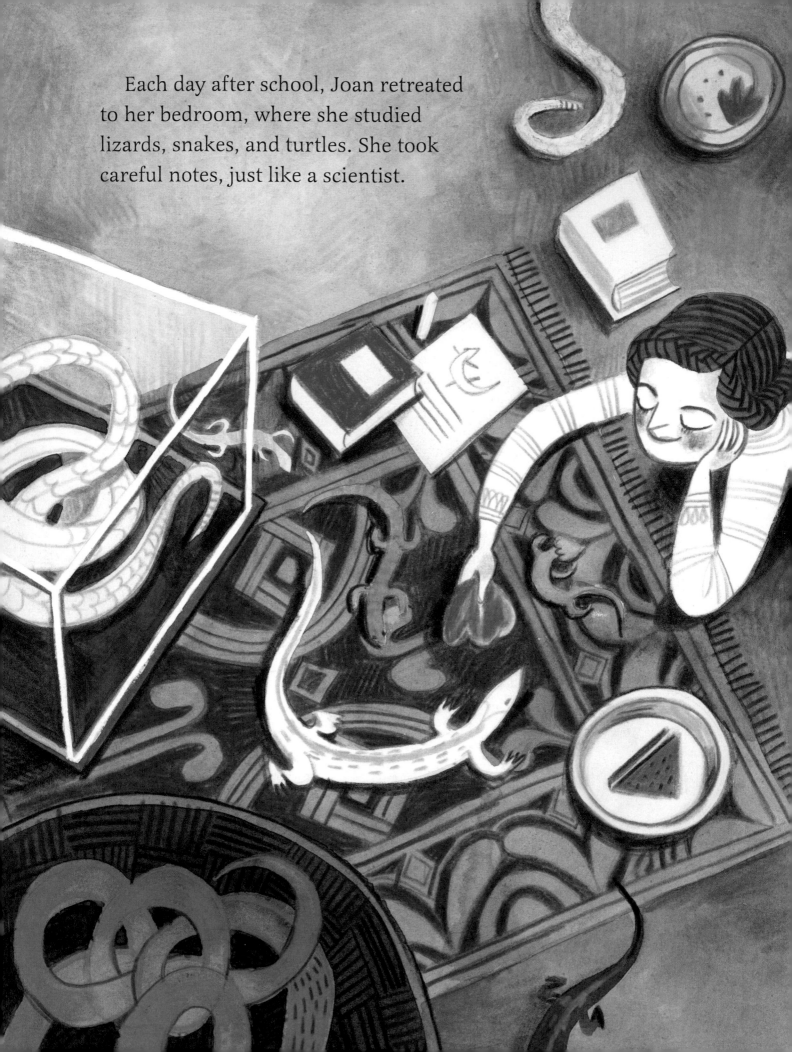

Each day after school, Joan retreated to her bedroom, where she studied lizards, snakes, and turtles. She took careful notes, just like a scientist.

And on the days Joan was too sick to attend
school, tiny toes and eager eyes cheered her up.
The reptiles were quiet and watchful, just like Joan.

For her sixteenth birthday, Joan received
a most curious gift—a baby crocodile!
She tied a little ribbon around his
waist and took him for a walk.

She even brought him to math class one day.
The students shrieked!
The teacher recoiled!
Apparently, crocodiles were not welcome at school.

When Joan grew older, she skipped the parties and dances with her friends. Instead, she sought out the curator of reptiles and fish at the Natural History Museum.

There, Joan and the curator talked snake scales: size,
shape, texture, patterns, and even evolution. Sometimes
Joan smuggled in her crocodile, to the delight of the
curator. He knew right away that Joan was special.

But soon, these carefree days came to an end. England was at war. Women took up jobs left behind by men.

The curator found himself short-staffed at the museum, so he hired Joan as his assistant.

Joan flourished at the Natural History Museum. As a scientist, she surveyed the museum's vast collections and published research papers on pit vipers and pancake tortoises. As an artist, she created exquisite models and drawings for the reptile exhibits.

When the curator retired, Joan took over. Men returning from war were surprised to find a woman in charge, but times were changing, and Joan was leading the way.

A few years later, the London Zoo decided to replace its old, outdated Reptile House. The zoo director asked Joan to design a new home for the animals.

Joan knew exactly how to keep reptiles happy. She added elaborate lighting and state-of-the-art heaters that provided hot spots to keep the cold-blooded animals warm. She brought in plants and created artwork that mimicked each animal's natural environment.

Joan took extra care designing one enclosure in
particular. By this time, stories had emerged of a "fierce
man-eating lizard" with a long, forked tongue, living
on the faraway Indonesian island of Komodo.
It was rumored to be . . .

Thirty feet long! Faster than a motorcar!
Stronger than an ox! They called it the Komodo dragon.

The stories didn't frighten Joan.
She dreamed of studying the dragons up close.

On opening day of the new Reptile House, visitors packed the zoo.

They gawked at the geckos.

They peered at the pythons.

And they marveled at the monitors.

But when they reached Joan's
special enclosure, they gasped!
Two seven-foot-long lizards
stared back at them.

Real-life dragons!

Although the visitors were thrilled, Joan was concerned. One of the Komodo dragons, Sumbawa, did not look well.

To the shock of the zoo guests, Joan entered the enclosure.

She moved Sumbawa to the
reptile clinic with the help of six
nervous keepers.

The dragon let Joan clean a sore in his mouth with no
fuss at all. In fact, he thanked Joan by licking her face.
Joan thought Sumbawa was brave.
The keepers thought Joan was brave.

News of Joan and the Komodo dragons spread. Reporters flocked to the Reptile House with questions.

Had she ever been bitten?

Was she afraid of the dragons?

What kind of woman runs a reptile house?

Joan wished the reporters would ask about the animals instead.

Joan cared for each and every creature in
the Reptile House. From daily health checks to
delicate surgeries, her dedication and talent could
not be matched.

Scientists all over the world read about Joan's research, her clinical skills, and the success of the new Reptile House. She became an international sensation.

The Zoological Society of London invited Joan to present her
Komodo dragon research at a scientific meeting. As Joan took
the stage, she wheeled out Sumbawa, sitting freely atop a large
table. The audience squirmed in their seats.

Joan stroked Sumbawa's head and fed him a pigeon. He ate it
in one gulp.

Sumbawa wandered through the audience as Joan
explained that the reports of Komodo dragons were greatly
exaggerated: They could grow up to ten feet, not thirty.
They ran fast, but not as fast as a motorcar. They could be
fierce, but they were mostly gentle.

When Joan finished her presentation,
Sumbawa returned to her side. The
audience erupted in applause.

Joan's passion for reptiles never waned.
For the rest of her life, she could be found
walking or riding through the zoo, with
Sumbawa by her side.

And just like when she was a little girl, Joan often
hosted children's tea parties at the Reptile House with
her scaly friends. Sumbawa was the guest of honor.

JOAN BEAUCHAMP PROCTER (1897–1931)

Joan Beauchamp Procter was born in 1897 in London, England, to Joseph and Elizabeth Procter. She began collecting lizards and snakes when she was ten years old. Instead of a favorite doll, Joan always brought along her favorite pet, a large Dalmatian lizard.

Joan attended St. Paul's Girls' School in London, but due to a chronic intestinal illness, she missed a large portion of school. Still, Joan was a very bright student. When she was sixteen years old, she received a small crocodile as a gift. She brought the crocodile to school with her, much to the dismay of her mathematics teacher.

Joan and her crocodile, Ramases

Joan sought out Dr. George Boulenger, curator of reptiles and fish at the Natural History Museum, then a part of the British Museum, when she needed an expert's advice concerning her reptiles. Dr. Boulenger was so impressed by Joan that he invited her to be his assistant after she finished school. This arrangement worked out well for Joan, since her poor health left her unable to go away for college.

Joan excelled at the Natural History Museum, presenting her first scientific paper on pit vipers when she was only nineteen years old. Four years later, upon Dr. Boulenger's retirement, Joan took over his duties. She was a remarkable herpetologist (a scientist who studies amphibians and reptiles). Her knowledge of reptiles and her artistic abilities allowed her to create magnificent exhibits while she pursued her scientific research.

Following her success at the Natural History Museum, Joan was appointed to the post of curator of reptiles at the London Zoo in 1923. There, she designed the new Reptile House, which featured the latest technology available to help maintain a stable environment for its inhabitants. Joan also included a reptile clinic in the design. She became well known for performing delicate surgeries on the eyes and mouths of dangerous animals, including crocodiles and pythons.

Soon after joining the London Zoo, Joan received exciting news from Dr. Malcolm Smith, a herpetologist at the Natural History Museum: Dr. Smith and the governor of the Dutch East Indies had reached an agreement to ship two Komodo dragons to the London Zoo. Little was known about Komodo dragons at the time, other than rumors of their extreme size and vicious nature. Joan quickly designed a custom enclosure for the dragons in the Reptile House. She installed special heated rocks, a large cave, and a swimming pool.

The two male dragons, named after Indonesian islands near Komodo Island, Sumba and Sumbawa, were the first live specimens to reach Europe. After the long boat trip, the dragons were in rough shape. Joan nursed their wounds, and the dragons appeared to appreciate her work. They were much gentler than expected, and Sumbawa, in particular, developed a strong connection with Joan. They took walks together through the Reptile House. Eventually, Joan and Sumbawa took walks outside together. Joan would steer Sumbawa with his tail. Sumbawa often attended children's tea parties at the zoo.

Joan presented her observations of Komodo dragons at the Scientific Meeting of the Zoological Society of London on October 23, 1928. Sumbawa accompanied her and walked freely through the audience during her presentation.

Joan's chronic health problems began to worsen at this time. She was in pain most days, but she managed to keep up with the daily activities of the Reptile House. At age thirty-four, Joan passed away in her sleep due to complications from her chronic illness. Until the end of her life, visitors to the zoo often saw Joan riding in her wheelchair while Sumbawa walked alongside her.

And to this day, if you visit the London Zoo, just inside the Reptile House, you'll find a marble bust of Joan, keeping watch over all the creatures inside.

KOMODO DRAGONS

The Dutch zoologist Peter Ouwens, director of the zoological museum in Java, first described Komodo dragons (*Varanus komodoensis*) in 1912. These carnivorous (meat-eating) monitor lizards were named for the Indonesian island on which they were discovered. Komodo dragons belong to the class Reptilia, along with crocodiles, snakes, turtles, and other lizards. They are considered the largest living species of lizard in the world, with males growing up to eight and a half feet long and females growing up to seven and a half feet long. On average, males weigh 175 to 200 pounds, while females weigh 150 to 160 pounds. The largest Komodo dragon found in the wild measured over ten feet long and weighed 366 pounds! They have a life expectancy of about thirty years in the wild.

The first live specimens of Komodo dragons arrived in Europe to great fanfare in 1927 and were exhibited at the Reptile House of the London Zoo. Joan Procter made many of the early observations on Komodo dragons, revealing that the dragons were not as vicious as many claimed.

BIBLIOGRAPHY

Bailes, Howard. "Procter, Joan Beauchamp (1897–1931)," *Oxford Dictionary of National Biography*. London: Oxford University Press, 2004.

Boulenger, E. G. "Obituary: Dr. Joan B. Procter." *Nature,* October 17, 1931: 664–665.

"Dragons at the Zoo. Two New-Comers Very Particular About Diet." *The Manchester Guardian*, June 16, 1927: 20.

"Dragons, Monsters in the East Indies." *The Times,* August 10, 1926: 15.

"English Woman Charms Snakes. Joan Procter, 25 Years Old, Has Charge of Reptiles in the London Zoo." *The Winnipeg Tribune*, August 15, 1923: 19.

"A Fat 'Dragon,' Thinning Treatment at the Zoo." *The Times*, March 2, 1929: 17.

MacBride, E. W. "Obituaries." Proceedings of the Linnean Society of London, 1931–32 (1933) 144: 183–185.

Mitchell, Chalmers. "Reptiles at the Zoo. Opening of New House To-day. Komodo 'Dragons.'" *The Times,* June 15, 1927: 17.

"Obituary: Miss Joan Beauchamp Procter." *The Manchester Guardian*, September 21, 1931: 10.

"Obituary: Miss Joan Procter, a Zoologist of Genius." *The Times*, September 21, 1931: 14.

Pinkley, Virgel. "Girl Manages Reptile House in London Zoo." *Mount Carmel Item*, December 28, 1929: 4.

Procter, Joan B. "Dragons That Are Alive To-day." Chapter IV of vol. 1 of *Wonders of Animal Life*. Edited by J. A. Hammerton (Waverly Book Company Ltd., London, 1928–29): 32–41.

Procter, Joan B. "On a Living Komodo Dragon *Varanus komodoensis*. Ouwens, exhibited at the Scientific Meeting, Oct. 23, 1928." Proceedings of the Zoological Society of London, 1928: 1017–1019.

"The Progress of Science. Electrical Heating for Reptiles, the Zoo Experiment." *The Times*, August 2, 1926: 13.

"A Quest for 'Dragons.'" *The Manchester Guardian,* August 4, 1926: 14.

"Snakes Alive and a Lady Who Loves Them. London's Curator of Reptiles." *The Advertiser* (Adelaide, Australia), January 4, 1930: 13.

"Women in the News—A Curator at the Zoo." *The Manchester Guardian*, July 21, 1923: 8.

"Zoo Loses Rare Reptile. Death of a Giant Lizard, Docile 'Sumbawa.'" *The Observer,* February 4, 1934: 26.

"ZSL Celebrates Dr. Joan Procter for International Women's Day." *ZSL London Zoo,* March 7, 2014: zsl.org/zsl-london-zoo/news/zsl-celebrates-dr-joan-procter-for-international-womens-day.

The Reptile House included displays of several amphibian species, too. Shown here are a few of Joan Procter's original paintings of the creatures she cared for, including *Atelopus varius*, also known as the clown frog.

Fig 10.2

Dorsal
scales

Cycl

Keele